"Carpe diem, quam minimum credula postero"

—Horace

ALSO BY MICHAEL PERKINS

<u>Fiction</u>
Evil Companions (1968, 1992, 2002)
Dark Matter (1996, 2001)
Burn (2002)

<u>Literary Criticism</u>
The Secret Record (1977, 1992)
The Good Parts (1994)

<u>Travel</u>
Walking Woodstock (with Will Nixon, 2009)

Carpe Diem

NEW AND SELECTED POEMS

Michael Perkins

© Cookie Kinkead

Carpe Diem: New and Selected Poems
Copyright © 2011 by Michael Perkins

Cover and book design by Melissa Mykal Batalin
Cover artwork by Ann Pachner

Published by Bushwhack Books • bushwhackbooks.com

Printed in the United States of America
The Troy Book Makers • Troy, New York • thetroybookmakers.com

To order additional copies of this title visit www.tbmbooks.com

ISBN: 978-1-61468-0093

for SONDRA HOWELL

and
Rena, Nathaniel, Theo, Stephanie

CONTENTS

ALMANAC

GIFT OF CHOICE

ACKNOWLEDGEMENTS

I would like to express my deep gratitude to my friend Henry Weinfield for his counsel and encouragement over the forty years when these poems were written; and to Joshua Coben, Sherry Kearns, Will Nixon, Allen Mandelbaum, Eric Waldemar, Richard Carella, and Burt Kimmelman for their responses to this work. The late Janine Pommy Vega, Mikhail Horowitz, and Janice King listened to early versions through many a delightful evening. William Bronk heard most of them.

I am grateful to the editors who first put them into print.

CARPE DIEM

NEW POEMS

FAR BEYOND

Far beyond those cloistered
Regions of the mind in which
Distracted reason seeks solace;
Far beyond the winter sky
The color of breath that figures
 In your dreams like prophecy;
Above the roar of eternity's vast mills;
In that land where things begin
Out of things transformed

I look for you.

CREDO

I believe in what I wake to,
A mood, the weather, the first word,
Or a kiss.
I believe in brevity
And the daily surprises
Of simple destinations:
The far green countries where
My legs have carried me;
The transgressed borders
Of regions off the map.
I believe in the hunger
Of what occupies me,
The glow of attraction
Helpless as a firefly in the dark.
I believe in the transcendence of trees,
And the metaphysics of fire:
I affirm the stability of bees,
And the persistence of desire.

SECRET AGENT

Unselfish inwardness, cloak me
In the invisible, dress me
In garments of transparency;
I would pass among the self-speakers
Like water in a frosted glass.
I would be other than what the world sees.

THE WHITE ROSE

I am dumb before
The fusillade of fireworks
That is the world; before
Its grim cacophony of disasters.
Henceforth I will live without
Tongue for utterance, without ears
For the harrowing clamor of time.

Perhaps then in some chamber,
In some inmost garden,
A door will open
In the confusion of my soul,
Clarity spreading its solace
Like sunlight after rain.
In this secret garden
I will seek the white heart
Of silence.
In the maze of confusion
That is my soul, I will find
One rose.

For Nana

NOSTALGIE DE LA BOUE

When I was young
And full of joyful noise,
I would run all night
With the barefoot boys.

In those Edenic times
Each day I breathed was bliss.
I bestrode the rolling earth
The way gods do—
By hanging onto humans
Whenever I came across them.

It seems so long ago—
Those merry saurian days
Before the rowdy rivers ran
Icy in their classic virtue,
Before chaste stars were hung
In the smoky tilted night,
When mountains still floated
Above the earth, millennia
Before the assumption of age.

THE WHISPER OF THE WINDLESS WAVE

After many countries and towns,
Disappointments and victories,
I come again to the sea.
Sitting by its restless side
Watching the rhythm of its tides,
I think of what long sustains,
And of much joy of living, what remains.

This I see from what I've done:
What comes will go, what goes will come.
It seems so little to have learned;
But it was mine, and hard earned.
The surf goes out, and it returns.

For Jacqui and Deborah

THE DOUBLE

I know he's out there
Pretending to be me—
Telling people all my lies,
Signing my name to checks
Made out to the Devil,
Ruining my credit
With the righteous;
But what am I to do?
You can't shoot your shadow.
You must endure his hangovers
And misdemeanors. You have
To stand up for him
When the lynch mob comes.
You have to agree when friends
Say you look alike. He is,
After all, my brother—
And I get to sleep with his wife.

GUILTY OF EVERYTHING

Whatever it is you want
To say about me, go right
Ahead: I confess that
I am guilty of everything.
If there is a crime I'm not
Accused of, let me claim it.
If there's sin I can atone for,
Send that snake to my cold bed.
I'd rather be deemed bad
Than think virtue was all I'd had.
My aim was to live it all
Before I heard the last call.
And I got what I wanted:
In sin and guilt I exceeded.

HOMAGE TO CYPRIS

If you believe, as I do,
That sensual pleasure
Is the highest good,
And chastity is a sin
Against the goddess Cypris:
If you believe, as I do,
That love is seeing yourself
In another person.
If you know, as I do,
That death is defeated only
By intensity of living:
Then you will enter tonight
Into your bedroom prepared
For worship of the kind
That will grant eternal life.
It is only through the body
That we are admitted to heaven.

LIGHT AND DARK

I will praise with open eyes
And celebrate what all despise:
The darkness by which is revealed
All that the light concealed.

For Marco Vassi, In Memoriam

PREDESTINATION

After a lifetime of this and
Then that, each wayward *next!*
Prescribed by ancient text,
I gazed without illusion
In the dark mirror of conclusion.
There, from cat calls to pratfalls,
I watched my life unfold
Like a comedy foretold.

A SHOUT

I am not my name,
Nor my biography.
I am not what you see—
Nor what I seem.
I am a breath, a dream;
I am words crossed out,
A whisper, a cry. A shout.

OLD FRIEND FROM FAR AWAY

I must have sipped a river
Of wine since I saw you last!
Come, fill your glass
Before we dine on remembrance.
Tell me where you've traveled,
And the women you've bedded.
I fear that my own life has unravelled,
And I've become what we dreaded:
A strange old man in dire circumstance.
I thought we'd built our lives to last;
How has it come to this so fast?

THE JOKE

Life is dangerous, we know;
And it *is* terminal. So we go.
Yet I still insist
It is not serious.
The worst will come, oh yes;
As will the best. It is all
Up to us, whether we laugh or cry;
Rather than some comforting lie,
Tell me a joke when I'm ready to die.

For Robert Stein

COMES THE REVOLUTION

We were partying down in hell
The night heaven fell.
The darker angels were shooting craps
And the Jezebels were dancing laps;
The news was so shocking we screamed.

This was more than we had dreamed:
We had conquered heaven by default,
And brought the world to a halt.
Now it was our responsibility
To rule wisely in eternity.
First we killed the gods; now God Himself,
Defeated by us, was on the shelf.
It was up to us to manage mankind.
The first thing we did was strike them blind.

HISTORY LESSON

When we think of what went before,
We recall the players, as if
Their names mattered any more
Than the names of characters
In books: markers in time's drift,
To remember what happened,
And make sense of the plot
By listing the actors.
(As if the who would give us the what.)
But the past will keep its mystery:
There is nothing to be learned from history.

For Sherry Kearns

IMMORTAL LONGINGS

In old photographs we are
Immortal dreamers—
Frozen in time, but
Projecting a life force
That wears us like clothing
To be discarded. Even after
We are ashes and wormfood,
Lost in the final forgetting
When all who knew us are gone,
Our red eyes caught by cameras
Still look upon this earth
With immortal longing.

For David Haber

A PRAYER BEFORE DYING

There is a reason for birth
Beyond this season on earth.
Before I meet the Reaper
I want to go much deeper
Into the dark cave of being
Where dying is a way of seeing.

Gods, grant me patience
As you once did insouciance.
I will sing your praises commanded
And perform the tasks demanded.
Just breathe me with your breath
As you lead me to my death.

TRAVEL ADVISORY

The past is a cannibal country
Where only the dead are happy.
Those who go there on a journey
Return hollow eyed and beaten.
Some stay there, and are eaten.

THE UNSEEN WORLD

At the funeral I could not cry.
I will leave the weeping to you.
Don't ask me for tears;
That well is long dry.
I will step outside and seek
The cold wind that polishes
The distant indifferent stars.
How the unseen world beckons!

In Memoriam, Linda Gabriel

DARK INVITATION

If you would come to me, bring yourself.
I will accept no substitutes.
You need bring no gifts other
Than those you were born with.
Come to me in the dark,
The only light that in your eyes.
Come softly singing
And I will greet you
As if we'd never parted,
As if we both yet lived.

THE EMPEROR OF AIR

I was a gladiator of grief,
The target of sharpened knives
In over a dozen lives:
Now I have lost the sun
With so much left undone.
Seeing that our lives were theater
And that the time given is brief,
I pressed down hard on the accelerator.
Now I am here, who once was there.
I have become an emperor
Who must live on air.

APOLLO, RISING

On a sunless morning
In a dark season
When I saw no reason
For greeting another day,
I lay down by a waterfall
On a shining stream under
A shade tree glistening,
And I had this dream:
There was a ladder I was
Climbing up from a world like
A scream which no one was hearing.
Rung by careful rung
I ascended until I reached
The sky where clouds are hung.
There I found Apollo, just
Rising from his golden bed.
"Like a city sacked, its
Towers toppled, so am I
Overcome by you," I said.
It was but a moment,
Or so it seemed. Time enough
For cities and thrones and powers
That be to rise to the clouds
And fall to the sea, in showers
Of angry retribution.

continued

But Apollo smiled, and I
Awakened by a waterfall
On a shining stream, my
Determination unshaken.

For Joshua Coben

DEAR FRIENDS

This is a letter I should
Have mailed when we were closer,
Before I got old and forgot
That our hot times would turn cold.
I should have said to you then
That no matter where or when,
I will come when you call.
I will stand with you when all
Curse your name and are unjust:
I will love you from here to dust—
For I think of you more than you know.
I go unseen with you where you go.
You are my better angels,
And I, your obedient servant, ask:
Forgive me—and write to me.

For Harold Wit

THIS IMMORTAL

Before the beginning of years, I was:
After my disappearance, I will be.
This life is not enough to contain me.
I shall walk through eternity
Looking for good company.
This life that lives inside me
Is immortal, and will always be.
So the god tells me; and I am free.

In Memoriam, Janine Pommy Vega

PERMIT ME PASSAGE

My past is uncharted and vast.
My future is just a guess.
I sleep with one eye open
And pull my boots on fast.
When I dream I always fly,
And when I wake I crash.
I come from what never was
And go to what forever is,
Perhaps I'll never die.
Permit me passage…..

CLOSER TO THE BONE

(2007)

To William Pachner

CLOSER TO THE BONE

So much to say, but
Not enough tongues to say it:
What eyes could not utter
What hands could not convey.

So much yet to say—
And everyone to hold,
Come will or ought or may.
Such stories left untold!

Here we are in this shining world,
Then here no more, so much left to say
Unsaid.

AT SIXTY-FIVE

I have rooms for rent
Inside my head,
Which strangers occupy
Who claim to know me.

They leave cryptic notes
In old diaries I don't read,
Inside shoes I don't wear.

Sometimes one kisses me
From inside and I smile—
Knowing what's to come.

I go dark with delight.

Sometimes one holds a gun—
Like an argument I'd forgotten.

The strangers have come.
Look this way for one.

VANITAS

This was me, the voice in the old book said.
Once I was studied, once I was closely read.
And these lines of print, written in a garden
By the September sea, were addressed
To one I thought to immortalize
In my summer vanity. Now I sit
On a dusty shelf, shut and silent,
And God knows she has forgotten me.

ADVICE

Do not waste yourself
On serious matters.
The world is well stocked
With busybodies,
Show-offs and saints,
Martyrs and mad hatters,
Do-ers and strivers,
Helpers and hurters;
Reputation is for fools.
The mean man looks to others
To find himself.
The superior man looks inside
And laughs to see a clown.

IN A VERMONT CEMETERY

No one of mine lies here
Beneath the frozen ground,
But I too have lived
A shadow's life, and carry
In my chest a valid passport
To the dark kingdom of the dead.

No one I loved is here
Suspended under earth,
But on a cold April day
When no one is about,
I like to walk among
The marble slabs, a countryman
Of the dreams beneath,
Aimlessly searching for spirits
Who remember being—
And still long for it.

THE SEVENTH SECRET

Say the first is in your pockets,
Where it serves to warm your hands.
The second is on the back of your tongue
Lying in wait for the unwary ears
Of innocence. The third is always
On its way somewhere else, seeking
To elude definition. And the fourth
Secret? That's easy. That's why it's
A secret—easy always is.
You can guess the fifth secret
When you look out the window and see
Sun on snow. Everything melts.
The sixth is that horn growing
From your forehead. Yes, that one.
This leaves the seventh, in which
Everything stands revealed.
Can you see it now?

For Djuna

O LORD OF DARK PLACES

I have arrived at age
Without defense,
And nothing now threatens
To make perfect sense.
So I come to you with urgency,
As my kind is like to do,
Having fallen into errancy,
Where only the reverse is true.

O lord of dark places,
I bow to you in fealty,
I accept your dominion wholly,
For I fear the end of feeling.
Great god of shadows, comfort one
Who has fallen into errancy.
I have arrived at age without defense.
Nothing now promises
To make perfect sense.

ABSENT FRIENDS

All my friends have gone away
To warmer places, above ground
And below, and winter winds
Blow news of a bleak future.
I sit with my books for company,
Recalling the splendid days
Gone by so quickly, when we
Danced in the sacred fires
Of immortal youth, and drank
The hot black milk of Eros.
Secrets we shared forgotten,
Promises we made unkept.
Shaken with regret for what
Was left undone, I lift my
Chipped wine glass and salute
Those dear companions
I long to see again.

THE DISTANCE

What a strange road it was
From coming in to going out
The time between first cry
And final shout so brief
Yet immeasurable.

When I thought I was found
I was always lost, somewhere else;
And now I see I ran all the way.

For Leslie

DISAPPEARANCE

Let me disappear as I once appeared;
No reason why, no reason not.
On the other side to be greeted
With cries of welcome, as I was here.

Let me disappear as we all will—
Having eaten too much and
Skipped out on the bill.

Let me disappear, back to where
I came from, so that I may come again
To you—like a trembling in the air.

I COULD WALK ALL DAY

(2002)

"I SAY THE ROSE..."

I say the rose you gave me owns
The hand that took it from you.
I say the tall willow
I linger under owns
The sky that feeds it.
Possession can be quantified.
I believe the green leaf
Eats the body of the sun.

As I know this old house
Owns my living inside it,
And I know the music I hear
Owns the ears I give it,
So I know possession.
I cannot be possessed
And will not be owned by another.
But something in me, like something
In you, possesses us both.

NATURAL FORCES

What you bring to me
I cannot take away.
We hold it together,
Like two carrying a sofa
Up many flights of stairs,
Or a man and a woman
Diving to kiss underwater.

We are forces visiting earth,
Like lightning and thunder,
Crackling and clapping and dancing
And then flickering away.

ONCE

It is our second autumn
And the leaves are turning
In Amherst, Massachusetts.
Late afternoon sun,
Red brick houses.
You start our Ford
With a screwdriver.
Later, we make love
In a cheap motel.
We are still young,
And will live forever.

ENTERING THE BEAUTIFUL ROOM

We are here at last,
Across from each other
In the beautiful room
We have walked through
In every previous life.

The windows are open
To the sound of the sea,
The room is full of sky.
It is almost too bright
To see into your eyes.
There is a voice singing,
Not sadly but purely,
Flowing through forever
In the beautiful room.

It is to live in this room
That we are born again…

POEM ON A LINE BY AKHMATOVA:
"I'M NOT YET CURED OF HAPPINESS"

Some dawn I will wake up laughing
So crazy in love with morning
I will keep from it my dreams
And bury nightmares in the sheets.

One morning I will open the great atlas
Of places I've never been and walk inside;
Off again, out of his head, some will say—

But heedless down the road I shall dance
A fine Welsh jig, headed out into
Those regions that lie
So far beyond sadness there is no echo.

So it is here we part, you marching alone
Into the swamp of despondency.
I have no sorrow left, and have
Forgotten the forlorn excuses of despair.

When I bid you farewell,
I will wave and force out a tear,
Careful to cover my mouth
In case it's drawn to smile.

For Ivory Robinson

AUBADE

On the morning of my death
I awoke as usual to the light.
I took a deep breath
And closed the door upon the night.
I rose and went about my chores,
Opening and closing other doors.
Everything was the same:
Here was my face, here was my name.
There was no fear.
I was still there.

EL DESDICHADO (AFTER NERVAL)

I am anthracite, pitch-dark but shiny,
Like the spot under the devil's tail.
Scorpions are my hook-tailed familiars.

Where I go I scream my curses into song;
I play on Orpheus's lyre Eurydice's lament.

In the shadow of inglorious deeds I lurk,
Unlucky, unfortunate, good for nothing,
The hermit of the blind alley, the saint of wrong;
The light of my life has gone out.

In memory of William Bronk (1918-1999)

SHADOW IS ALL

Substance fades with sundown,
Evening deepens the shades
Left by the dramatic afternoon.
The fabled river lies dreaming
Curled up to the dappled shore.
Everywhere shadows are rubbing
Shapes into flickering life.
Nothing is forbidden now
But the illusion of light.
This is what lies inside the dark,
This final evening that fades
All substance into shades.

THE WELCOME

When the last mourner has departed
And the sweet sad singing no longer
Defies the silence of forever,
The eyes of the dead, closed by life,
Slowly open on a darkness
That is not dark—as if the center
Of the night were lighted
By the passage of the soul
From its temporary home
In the sanctuary of the soil.

The eyes open when the last
Mourner has left, and see
With infant clarity
The incredible unsayable splendor
Of the world that opens its arms
And offers welcome home, once again.

In memory of Connie Markle

THE DAY'S SIGN OF FOREVER

Embrace the morning's mood
With a readiness to play.
Open your heart to the weather.
Look in the alphabet of trees
For the day's sign of forever.

Look up at night for the stars,
Scanning the vastness for home.
Welcome sleep. Wade into your dreams.
Drift in the river of time
Back to the source of what seems.

And between morning and night,
Love whatever you choose
With all your distracted might.

This is all there is—
Readiness and mood,
Search and surrender.

THE GRAMMAR OF NECESSITY

I blame it on the books,
Those oracles of chance
In whose pages we happen
Upon our future selves.

The sentences led the way
Through the unspoken,
And the books followed:
Each word arranged to make sense
Of being here, alive like this,
Looking out at the bright sun.

At last each of us is owned
By our words and the sentences
We have imposed upon ourselves;
By the inexorable
Grammar of need, and the
Iron laws of reversal,
Recurrence and certain closure.

We are possessed by language:
Our mouths are forced open by it,
Our vocabularies betray
Our most recondite display.

continued

No one escapes his words;
Even in the final
Subterranean refuge,
The syllables rise up in our throats.

For Henry Weinfield

MANEUVERS

The lines march across the pages
Like columns of men in single file
On a mission to retake the past.

Autumns when we walked the Great Beach,
Summer evenings under the shade tree.
So few lines to hold so many memories.

For Viki

THE SWEEPER
(Jardin, San Miguel de Allende)

At five in the morning,
In the garden beneath
The blue jacaranda
Where the peacocks scream
And the fountain refreshes
The riotous flowers,
I sweep the blue shreds of dawn.

I sweep the drowsy scorpions
From the rumpled bed of morning
So the day is easy
And without apprehension.

I sweep the crumbs from the picnics
Of the poor, so they will not seek
Second helpings of what they cannot have.

At five in the morning
No one is here to hold
The great bunches of balloons
And the April rain has washed
Away the *cantilena* of the guitars
And the triumph of the bright horns.

For Stella Chasteen

I HAVE NOT HEARD

I have not heard, as I'd hoped,
The magic Mayan Quetzal
Sing in Guatemala. Nor
Do I think now I will ever
Climb into the wet jungles
Listening for its elegant
Exuberant call.

I'll never ride the high country
On a fast horse by moonlight,
Nor lead a raiding party
Into a sleeping coastal village.

These are boys' dreams of adventure,
Stored in attics everywhere,
Memorials of imagined lives
That never could have been.
Sometimes I visit them.

For Colin

THE QUALITY OF INDIRECTION

As self-defining as water
Springing freshly from the earth,
Or sunlight on a winter's morning
Spreading its long slow fingers
Across the great shadowed lawn,
It is the quality of indirection
To seem to lose itself
In its own delayed surprise—
Yet to cover ground as surely
As dawn widens in our eyes,
When dreams of shaken splendor
Are the sole remains of all
Our midnight certitudes.

For Richard Carella

DREAM

As I grow, so will I go
On the path of least intent,
Stepping fast and stepping bold
Past the goat in the basement
And the rat struggling in the box
That I know I cannot hold.

This the dream foretold:
The future that waits
Buried in the falling snow
Lies past the goat in the basement
And the rat struggling in the box
That I know I cannot hold.

ORIGINAL FACE

"What was your original face,
before you were born?"

- Zen teaching

Cleaning the mirror by moonlight,
I uncover the first of my faces,
Hidden from myself all these
Dissembled years. The portrait
Is out of focus at first,
Still new; but I can see
That it's unsympathetically true.
As I watch, it gathers the many
Into the unknown One—
And it is too late to wish
I had not begun.

For Janice King

ALMANAC

1997

To Mikhail Horowitz

JANUARY

Sound the curled horns, beat muffled drums,
Commence anew the cavalcade of days:
It is nineteen ninety-seven.

The soft rhythm of snow plays
On the swaying birches, and
The blue pond is filled with clouds.
The vault of heaven is the color of grief.
Our valley is ice-locked.
                    It is the wolf month.

Who lives alone in winter woods
Is a stranger to himself.

It is time, as the world opens me,
To go looking
For the god of beginnings,
Who parts the curtains of sky at dawn.
It is time for his cold breath
In my lungs:
The inspiration
And suspiration
Of the god who looks both ways,
And breathes me everywhere.

FEBRUARY

The shroud of winter falls
Over the sleeping mountains.
The town is shut,
Its windows sealed,
Its roads blocked.

It is the month of expiation,
The time of birds mating
And kale sprouting.
From the ends of the earth
Strong winds come to crack the trees.

MARCH

The sun comes and goes
As if someone were playing
With the lights in a dark room.

The ants send out scouts
To reconnoiter our cupboards.
The first wasp infiltrates
And staggers on the window sill.

Every day the radio reminds us
That Mars is the god of war
And March is his month.

For Zachary

JUNE

Summer solstice, the wheel of the year turns.
On the longest day of the year
We dine outside, under the pink blossoms
Of the shade trees, drinking too much wine.
The full red moon shines down on our happiness.

JULY

The corn is low in dry fields.
Bugs bite bare legs still winter-white.
A snapping turtle swims laps
In the pond below Tonshi's crest.
Bicycle riders whiz past,
Summer fireworks *sput* and *fizz.*
Sweat trickles in the humid evening.
Soon there will be a wedding;
I am father of the bride.

AUGUST

Rain at last, although too little,
And the green tongues are not slaked.
The mountain road at midnight
Is a tunnel through the trees
To the top, where I look up
To watch the Perseids fall
Across the endless sky.
In the morning, huge black clouds;
Hailstones sharp in the afternoon road.

SEPTEMBER

Where the fist of the Cape curls,
Our small plane climbs above clouds
And everything is shining.
There, we see, is Provincetown,
And look! the round Wellfleet ponds.
What is hidden on the ground
Lies revealed from above.
We see our landscape whole
With another kind of love.

For Bill Markle

OCTOBER

The soft gift of morning
Is slowly pulled
From the magic sleeve of dawn
And shaken, so that
The dusty golden hills
Of California
Unwrap themselves
From our eyes.
At Harbin Hot Springs
There are bubbles left
By last night's bathing.

In memoriam, Kathy Acker

DECEMBER

Eight planets in a line in the southwest:
Omens in the sky as the year ends,
Not to be seen again for a century.
Overnight, snow closes its white gloves
On the surprised dry mouth of morning
And silence spreads everywhere.
Ah, vastness of snow, murmur of ice!

GIFT OF CHOICE

(1992)

To Charles Gatewood

I.

A serpent cloud swallowed morning
That is the child of night,
And Sam plunged surprised
Into the stream of forms,
Lost in black inside and out
—Not here, not there
Now here, now there—
Flickering like a candle
Losing the air.

Give back the light!
Sam cried, and fell down
And beat the earth for light,
Banged his head for light—and the
Lightning flashed inside him;
Then it was dark again.

II.

Sam saw what lay beneath sight—
His world emptied out of light,
While inside the spooky lightning
Struck and sizzled, and sent him
Spinning down into the deeper maze
Of self from which journey no Sam
Returns the same. Figure Sam
For a fool destined to disappear
Down a crooked line—but then,
If not for love of travel,
No marvelous arrival.

III.

Sam woke up in a black room,
The only light his life before,
Barely flickering in the gloom.
He stood up to look for a door
But his fingers found no knob,
No crack in the dark—no exit
From that familiar room
Anywhere but in anticipation.

IV.

It was here, the night had come
From which there was no further appeal,
And no more mornings left to shine
In the deep grab bag of days.
No more tedious afternoons
Arranging dots and lines
While outside the last glow
Of brightness surrendered
To the encroachment of evening.
Throw ink on those fading rays of sun
And pull down the shades of night:
The flight from day is done.

V.

Imagine a still black pool
In the center of a mountain
And see Sam floating there,
Upside down for certain.
Look up at the stars,
But make no sound.

VI.

Now let this new Sam be you.
Or better still, for this breath
Be Sam in everything:
Then it's not only his fingers
Clinging to the cliff,
It's not only his heel
Stepping on his own hand.
The next breath you take
Might be Sam's—who knows to say
What Sam might become
When he steps through
The beaded curtain of the dark?

VII.

Call Sam everyone who spent youth
In the subjunctive mood
Or as-if and would-that-it-were,
Of make-believe and metaphor.
Call Sam just what happened next,
As in those bold improvisations
Stamped in the shadow print of memory
Sam reveals the selves
He might have been
Before becoming partial Sam again.

VIII.

Something crazy crawled up his spine
And slipped into his head.
Something impossible
Called and fluttered there.
An old chaos filled his ears.
He heard the drumming roar of blood—
And did what the rhythm said.

IX.

Childhood for Sam was running
Down endless hallways
Slamming all the doors shut
And catching toes and fingers
And grown-ups in the act
Of making simulacra of Sam.
More selves to be! he cried.
The child in Sam could talk to stones
Whose hieroglyphic speech was news
A hundred thousand years ago.

Speaking the language of stones,
Same could feel silence settle
Cool and flat and final on his tongue.

X.

Sam decided that he would not
Endeavor to live beyond style.
It is the surface of the water
That pleases him most,
Its constant rippling changes.
He glides across the bay at sundown
And slips like a hand into
The green glove of forests
On the darkening shore,
Calling out an invitation
That will linger in the memories
Of those who wave back to him.

Sam decided that he would not
Endeavor to live beyond art,
That he would celebrate
All his beginnings and endings,
That he would follow the map
Of solitude tattooed in his genes,
That he would gladly eat the dark
That was offered to him by sundown
Beckoning across the glistening bay.

XI.

When society tired Sam
It was solitude that saved him,
Solitude he pulled like a sock
Over his head, solitude
That showed him how to
Still the longings that in his youth
Sent him searching in the night.

XII.

Sam didn't show his teeth to everyone,
So they said he smirked. But teeth to him
Were gates to raise and lower
Before his squatting tongue—
The plush seat of speech and sex,
The wet red genital,
The secret longing in every mouth.
Sam smirked to hide his tongue
And the constant desire
That lurked behind his teeth.

XIII.

Loving women as he did,
Sam hoped to suit one or two.
So down the line of ladies
He danced that old soft shoe—
Here and there pausing
To whisper in their ears
The words of some old love song
Written in him before he was born.
Certain of his life's task
He donned the lover's mask,
Hoping to find delight
Before he slept at night.

XIV.

When the night whispers
Its old invitations,
Sam sings to himself
Of turning again
As he has before,
Of jumping through a window
Or backing out a door.

Sometimes when the night
Swells with yearning,
Sam sings to himself
That he may yet fall
In step with any passing shadow
Who is more than passing fair.
He sings to himself
That he would still dare.

Sometimes when dawn breaks
He has not slept for singing
And falls back into a dream
Of running his thumb once more
Along a summer edge,
Of walking down the street
Bright as an exclamation mark.

How he shone in this deepest dark!

XV.

And yet sometimes the darkness
Seemed to wear on beyond weather;
Sometimes Sam could not forebear,
And his hands closed beseechingly
Around his own throat. Then
He wanted to stare into
The midday sun, he wanted
His umber world a blinding white
As he stumbled across his life.

XVI.

Sam sometimes longs for separation,
But open ground makes him dizzy;
So wake him when the leaving's done.
Let him slip off in sleep
—But don't forget to wake him
In the frozen ground.

XVII.

Of all the lives he'd led,
Sam knew he'd miss the last one most.
For the expansive worlds of Sam
Are bounded by the next breath,
And inspiration is a style of life
As sane as any other—for air
Is as unpredictable as light
And just as likely to be sucked away.

XVIII.

Nothing left to say,
Sam slouched through the park—
Hands jammed in his pockets
As if to pray:

Fingers spread out like
Spies in the dark.

XIX.

New Year's. Careless day dreams
Have swallowed another year.
All the delusions of adequacy
Have shaped Sam's life story.
The generations before him
Emerge from the darkened mirror.
At last what he saw
Was more than shadows on a wall.
At last what he heard
Was not only what he called.
Was this the face he'd settled for
In his argument with metaphor?

XX.

Morning pours its tintinnabulum
Of sounds and light into the fluttered eyes
And giant curled ear of sleep, while
Birds fuss about the coming storm.
There is a ringing in Sam's waking ears
That is the world calling him
To rise and answer it.
Another day, another chance
To beat the drum of self again,
With luck to move the lips
To praise and kiss with breath
What newly stirs inside.

XXI.

Sam knows a soliloquy
Is no place for him to shelter,
That he must walk bare-headed in the rain,
But sometimes he sang these songs
Of dark and light
And couldn't stop
Until he was completely
Out of breath…

XXII.

After long restless survival,
With more years than expectations left,
The time had come to revive
The art of graceful disappearance.

Nothing was left undone—
All his lovers were generous,
Beyond the grasp of opportunity;
And his hands brought to the tasks
Of living some gift of choice.

Now it was time to follow
Beyond posted schedules
The fading afternoon light,
And slip off the calendar
Like a stolen morning in spring
Spent sitting by a quiet stream.

PRAISE IN THE EARS OF CLOUDS

(1982, 2005)

"NOW THE FILIGREE RUINS OF WINTER"

Now the filigree ruins of winter
Sparkle in the fields of light.
I will praise the roundness of things,
The curve of growth,
The news of summer in the seed.

"WHEN IN GREEN WAYS I LIVED
MY CHILDHOOD DAYS"

When in green ways I lived
My childhood days,
            I ran
With rabbits and swam
With golden carp
In their stone pools;
All the mornings were mine,
And as many afternoons!
I climbed the tallest trees,
I chewed their magic leaves;
There were whole seasons
In which I did no more
Than learn to praise.
My gift to awake and see,
No one was more free—
When in green ways I lived
My childhood days.

"I COME FROM BLUE MOUNTAINS"

I come from blue mountains
And the pine beds
    Of mountain women.
There's moss in my hair,
    And white laurel there.

"IT IS SUMMER, AND ALL THE WORLD RULES ME"

It is summer, and all
The world rules me,
Every cloud and rock
And clump of earth:
Now my five senses lead me
To forsake my winter reasons—
And I will drift where I am drawn.

"BEYOND OUR MOTHER MOUNTAIN"

Beyond our mother mountain
And her rushing silver streams,
The autumn wolves are running.
String the wind-stripped trees
With nets of patience.
Hummingbirds suck the sweet
Small bones of Indian Summer.
The forest is a feast of absence.

"THE DAYLIGHT WORLD HAS PULLED ITS SHADES"

The daylight world has pulled its shades.
Light candles on the darkening grass.
As the wind blows them out
One by one, think of the sun, dying,
And of the moon's terrible bereavement—
Summer light, there will be
Crowds at your funeral:
We'll run through the streets
With torches, looking for you.

For William Bronk

"IN MY DREAMS THEY RISE AND FALL AGAIN"

In my dreams they rise and fall again,
Mountains I climbed as a boy,
Rivers I floated down with my friends.
In my dream I take up the brush
And let the dark rivers flow,
So again the mountains leap onto
The virgin rice paper, in ink
Dark as my hair at fifteen,
When my friends were still alive.

OVERLOOK MOUNTAIN INVOCATION

By god, you're a fine mountain,
Overlook, dancing with your sisters
In a ring around our valley,
South peak blue
      Against the northern sky!

Overlook, you are
Our farewell to houses!
Overlook, you are
Our entrance to heaven!

Great Overlook!
Open our eyes closed with coins –
Open our ears stuffed with traffic –
Open our hearts so long indifferent
To your geologic transcendence,
Great Overlook!

Admit us all who live at your knees
Into the ancient chambers of your
Immortal, marmoreal being,
Where we may be transformed
Into mountains ourselves,
      Great Overlook!

For Will Nixon

CLIMBING MOUNT GUARDIAN

In late June I climbed
      Mount Guardian,
Hoping that when I reached the summit
I might somehow keep on climbing.
On my way up a snake slid
Across my path and stopped,
Curved like a hook, to watch me pass:
A sign, I hoped, that I was
Still welcome in those green woods.
Higher up, the mountain laurel
Spread in pink bloom everywhere.
Below me the wide Woodstock Valley
Lay half in shadow, half in light.
A fly my sole companion,
I stood on a boulder near the top
Stretching up to the sun,
Shrinking in mountain perspective
All the little lives I led below.
Hawks swooped, an eagle passed,
And I felt the glad ache
In my shoulder blades where
      Wings would start.

For Scott Markle

"IN THE VALLEY I HOLD MY HEAD UP"

In the valley I hold my head up—
High, as a human being should.
After all, when you are on flat land,
Do as the flat-landers do: pretend
Nothing is higher than human.

But oh, to bow my head
To the low-ceilinged sky,
Home in the mountains again!

SPRING ON SLIDE MOUNTAIN

Late morning in early June:
Climbing fast up Slide Mountain,
Looking for the last of Spring
On its cloud-shrouded summit.

Hiking straight up the quartz path,
Stiff wind bending the balsams,
Wet gray curtains close the view
And sudden sunlight parts them.

Shoulders of lower mountains
Wear the pale green of May still.
Somewhere a red-tailed hawk
Condescends to bicker with crows.

We stop for rare Spring Beauties,
Trillium and Bunchberries;
Drink cold mountain water from
An iron pipe. Near the bottom,
Splash down a streambed
In late afternoon light:
One more perfect day snatched from death.

For Hera

"HERE BY SOME WHISPERED INVITATION"

Here by some whispered invitation,
No reservations, neither guest nor host,
Wandering like a sentence in the mind of God;
Keeping no secrets from the persistent rain
Or the inquisitive sun: my life is open
To the sudden interrogation of the wind,
And the manic interruptions of the moon.

THE PERSISTENCE OF DESIRE

(1977, 2004)

"I HAVE TASTED THE BLOOD OF TREES"

I have tasted the blood of trees.
I know the gnarled speech of leaves,
And the vocabulary of tools;
The scream of cedar against the saw.
I know the blunt emotions of wood.
Perhaps in this deep forest
I will come upon a woman
Who is savory as pine
And silvery as birch.

"HOW CAN I SAY"

How can I say
How she looks undressed?
Just say that in her clothes
She looks like other women
Who cannot be possessed.

Just say she's like the morning,
Brightening. Like the bare tree –
The only one in the forest
Who married lightning.

Just say she's on my fingers
And in my hair:
That a wild smell
Of devotion's
In the crackling air.

"I WANT THE CLOSED EYES"

I want the closed eyes
Of willingness,
The open knees
Of listening,
The polished thighs
Of experience;
I want the swollen
Nipples of satisfaction.
Then I want an end
To wanting; but
I would keep
A semblance of desire.

For V. K.

MIDNIGHT IN THE GARDEN

Bruise on her breast,
Not my fingertips,
Gloss on her lips,
Not licked from me.
Hair a tangled halo
I hadn't mussed,
Eyes swollen and wanton,
Not turned my way,
Her smell of lust
Stronger than sharpest memory;
I could not swallow,
I could barely see.
This was what it meant:
This was being free.

"A PIT IN THE BELLY OF A PEACH"

A pit in the belly of a peach,
A gnat in the eye of an elephant;
I haven't lacked for shelter
In this extempore life.
Neither have I questioned
The feast of pain
Or the sure hands
Of those who prepare it.
I've snatched kindness
From the mouths of crocodiles.

"THIS MORNING THE WORLD CAN ROLL TO HELL"

This morning the world can roll to hell
Like a rubber ball looking for a dog
Down a dead end street; I'm staying home.
I'll spend the day stretched flat in bed,
Doorbell disconnected, blinds drawn,
Hiding like a liar from the truth.

"I LOVED HER FLESH BECAUSE IT FILLED MY HANDS"

I loved her flesh because it filled my hands
With the gravity of her soft response.
But the nights we spent together were perishable.
The hot coals she brought to our bed are cinders.

"GIVE ME SOME NEWS OF HER, SAILOR"

Give me some news of her, sailor.
Tell me, is she queen of the lands
That smolder beyond the river?
If she is, I'll camp beside
Its currents in the night and take
From those luminary merchants,
The sellers of stolen light,
The comfort the abandoned know;
Like Orpheus, I'll float a candle
On that thick black water
Where the dreams of lovers flow.

In memoriam, Renie Perkins

"WHEN NOTHING REMAINS OF
WHAT MUST HAVE BEEN"

When nothing remains of what must have been,
And all that we love has vanished in smoke,
Solitude is the final strategy
To slow the turning wheel of time.

Solo, I can invent a past that never was.
Solo, I can embellish faded memories
Until they glow like sunlight on a pond.
Wrapped in a cloak of solitude,
I stroll down country lanes
Looking into every window for
A glimpse of what must have been.

For William Pachner

"OLD MORTALITY, I POLISH YOU"

Old mortality, I polish you
Like a fallen apple.
You are hard and wormy.
I spit on you to make you shine.
I hide you behind my back.

Michael Perkins is the author of six collections of poetry. *The Secret Record*, literary criticism, was published by William Morrow in 1976. Among his other works of fiction and non-fiction are the novels *Evil Companions*, *Dark Matter*, and *Burn*. His poems and essays have appeared in *The Village Voice*, *Younger Critics of North America*, *The Nation*, *Mother Jones*, *Paper*, *Notre Dame Review*, *Exquisite Corpse*, *Big Bridge*, *Talisman*, *Rain Taxi*, and *American Book Review*. He was the Leydig Trust's Writer of the Year in Great Britain in 2002; and he is the recipient of the 2007 Obelisk Award for Lifetime Achievement, and the 1957 Dunbar Poetry Prize.